Seasons Of Love

A collection of poems from the best year of
my life.

Carah Hwang

/ BookLeaf
Publishing

India | USA | UK

Made with ❤ on the BookLeaf Publishing Platform

www.bookleafpub.in

www.bookleafpub.com

Dedication

25 brought me back pieces of myself I never knew were missing.
As I turn another year older,
I am reminded of the importance of celebrating oneself.

Happy 26th Birthday!
This year brought the restoration of gifting from a generous heart.
You've earned back the joy of holidays, the peace that comes with justice, and genuine ecstasy.
I will treasure moments spent with *you*.
Your love is gifted, not guaranteed.
Cheers to a lifetime of learning <3

Preface

Beauty is everywhere.
But the shadows creep in and must be acknowledged.

These poems are the culmination of my being.
I hope equally that you find a small piece you can relate
to *and* that you never understand the labor of its birth.

Acknowledgements

divine timing, divine presence, and the little me who dreamt of a perfect world.

flirting with life

I write poetry to remember the best parts of my life.
I end up with lines and lines of half-baked thoughts that
makes sense to no one but myself.
I write page after page of personal references,
making sense *only* to an audience of one.

I wonder why I've been single all my life.
A part of me wants to blame it on my overly protective
parents or an inability to commit.
In those moments, I am reminded that *no one could ever
love me the way I love myself.*

They could never know...
the way I pick up a penny and flip it on its head for the
next person to inherit the luck.
The peaceful silence I've cultivated in my life.
How deeply *sexy* I feel when I take care of my body.
Because it's not just taking care of my body;
it's the overcoming of the kind of self-love that needed to
scream to be heard.
It came in the form of buying myself a ring that I wear
on the one that everyone was always waiting for *the one*
to come along and adorn.

I am here.

And the romance we find in this world isn't a cheap pair
of rose-colored glasses,
like the faint outline of glasses of wine on the pages of
my journal, which I find so utterly chic.
Like Hamilton who writes like he's running of time—
I was looking for something meaningful to write about.
It *all* is.
And my something-ness doesn't take away from your
someone-ness.
We are *everything*.

dream dragon

Last night, I dreamt of loss.
The loss of the deepest friendships I've ever known.
Or maybe I'm grieving the deepest parts of myself.
The loss of childhood innocence that had the ability to
care so deeply,
in a way that no longer makes sense.
But the carousel never stops turning.
I think——dreams are such a gift.
They are glimpses into lifetimes never known;
ones that my fragile heart could never bear.

kintsugi

/ˈkintsəgē,kintˈsōōgē/ noun

the Japanese art of repairing broken pottery by joining pieces back together and filling cracks with lacquer dusted with powdered gold, silver, or platinum.

In some cultures, when you chip a cup, you throw it away.
Fearing misfortune, you fail to see 99.9% of its remaining utility.
I am a chipped cup.
You looked at me and covered me in a red cloth.
I thought I was destined for the grave.
It felt like you took a hammer to my bones
and shattered me into tiny pieces.
You did it with such precision and premeditation;
I wondered how someone could do something so cruel.
But you didn't throw me away like I thought you would.
You took me into your shed,
where beautiful things are made.
You melted down pure gold and filled every broken
crevice of my aching soul.
You looked at me with such admiration and awe.
You placed me in the middle shelf of your kitchen
cupboard,

comfortably in arm's reach.

Every morning, you praise me.

And I am once again made whole.

my mother's hands

One day, I'll be sitting in my home, all alone.
It will smell like patchouli and jasmine,
bergamot and eucalyptus.
I'll have candles burning and dance naked in the soft
glow of the passing sunset.

And I will wish it smelled like the faint wafting of my
mother's cooking.

footloose

In another life, I was in a heavy metal band.
And the *rage* I hold inside my heart had a place to exist.
It would cut through the stillness and play with the
tranquility in the air.
My parents didn't ask me why I didn't go to church on
Sunday,
or forbid me from listening to "secular" music.
My dad brought home an exciting, new record and we
blasted it freely throughout the house.
I don't keep my phone on silent or watch videos with the
volume off.
I'm not afraid to call my friends because my family
understood privacy.
And *propriety* never existed in my little universe.
No one commented on the black dress I wore to my 6th-
grade band recital,
or told me I was wearing too much makeup for my age.
As if smothering my eyelids in a bright turquoise paste
would somehow lead to teen pregnancy.
I was eight.
And lighting a candle isn't a silent act of rebellion.
It's the calling in of a new season.
One where the cool night air lulls me into dreams of fall,
pacifying my need for a little bit of romance.

American classics

I am blessed in this moment with a melancholy that
makes for good poetry.
A brooding sultry that is completely out of my control.
So much understanding and nothing left to say.
Pure eyes, pure heart.
And completely alone.
All of my child's deepest questions and fears,
answered.
All of my child's deepest dreams,
manifest.
Pulp Fiction suddenly makes sense.
Holding creation in my womb until it's ready to be
birthed——not one day too soon nor too late.
And truth does not need to be screamed,
only observed.
We don't need to *wake up;* we only need safe spaces to
express.

The old wives' tales spoken by word of mouth, from one
generation to the next, all around the world, almost
simultaneously, become true to you.
Like the invention of the wheel.
These sacred truths turned into cliches, fallen on ears
that were not quite ready to hear them.

Take your time, dear beloved.
When your own voice follows you throughout these 25
years, asking to be heard,
you can hug yourself tightly.
Let *one* in at a time.

Frankenstein's curse

To live ironically
is to look at yourself in a hall of mirrors.
Each passing glance sending you your karma.
There are shattered pieces on the ground,
forming this Creature of a thing——
created, never to find someone like him.
The *idea* of love dying with the Unnamed.
I run to put on my mask.
The human gaze can be so cruel.

the kind of love I make

The kind of love I have to offer...
does not entangle you.
The kind of love I have to offer doesn't show you the
way.
It stands firm in its sovereignty and offers you the same.
Let my love for you grow with each fleeting, shared
moment.
Let my love be based in reality and not the notion of one.
Let it give you the freedom to experience every version
of you that ever was and wanted to be.
Let my love for you conquer death.
It will forget the way you look sometimes because there
is no room for the mind when the heart is exploding
with reverence.
Let's let *newness* come with each word and experience.
I will give you pieces of me, wholeheartedly, without
judgment, expectation, or competition.
Like the giving tree, I will give you all of me.
Yet, I will still be whole.

my guru

Three years ago, I was sitting at the Sutro baths, listening
to Baba Ram Dass.
The audience erupted in laughter.

I didn't get it.

Today, I let out a roar;
I am elated by his laughter.

A mountain is just a mountain.

mastery

To give up your identity is to become a student again.
I search the clouds for a semblance of you.
In Pluto's pursuit of truth, I had forgotten just how
beautiful you are.
Drawing me closer and closer to destiny.
I find myself on the edge of the solar system.
I'm a planet, I'm not a planet.
Like a twisted game of *she loves me, she loves me not,*
I know *enough* and then nothing at all.
I am the student, again and again.
Oscillating between subject and object,
I emerge from the chains of fear.
How else can we know love?

the observer effect

Falling in love with life again.
It's the subtle appreciation
of the laugh-out-loud conversations overheard between
two strangers,
when you decide to listen in without joining in, or
showing a glimmer of your observation.
Or finding an artist you love,
with no *need* to see them in concert and somehow, make
it *yours*.
It's spending an hour talking to someone you've just met,
with no agenda.
I am transformed by their excitement to be seen;
and yet, we part ways with no idea if we'll ever meet
again.
There's a certain divinity in letting good things go.
To leave its perfection alone.

*It's bringing presence in every moment you once tried so
hard to escape.*

Particles rearrange when they are observed.
I encase the endless love I hold for you in a bubble,
only letting it graze you as it passes by.

So that I might see you in your infinite beauty, free of my own misunderstanding.

telephone

Words Matter.

A movement I've ruminated on my whole lifetime, and definitely in the last.

The purity of a passion project dedicated to learning a language they ruled "dead."

It was never dead; it was evolving.

much like us.

And sorcery becomes *source*-ery.

Amateur becomes *amare*——to love.

Casting a spell is simply worship.

Pagan, or *pagus*, meaning village.

And an attack on "political correctness" that buries the truth behind a love for all humans as equal.

Wouldn't you agree?

crab claw

The pure ecstasy of eating a meal,
unbothered;
by sound, by stimulation.
I feel the gentle heat of my home-cooked mushroom
guisado nip at my tongue.
I am reminded of the ease of a microwave, the luxury.
And maybe prayer can look like just one moment of
stillness before taking your first bite.
I am enjoying the leftover broth from my mom's birthday
dinner with her friends.
They took her out to shabu shabu.
What a beautifully human thing to ask and remember
your friends' birthdays.
To celebrate the life you get to share.
I see the leftover crab claw, floating in the soup.
I wondered if they played a little game of "who wants the
last bite."

sojourner

I feel more *settler*.
I used to long for *nomad;*
to be untethered to any one place, any one people.
The insatiable art of mastering people,
gathering stories from every corner of the world.
I longed for *more*——what was coming next.

I trapped a fly in my window blinds today.
I hoped it would die peacefully, without need for
violence.
I came to check on it hours later.
It had settled in the threshold between inner and outer.
There was no where left to go, *no place to hide.*

distortion

There are cameras all around us.
Like an episode of Black Mirror,
we are asked to look for a deeper truth than the one
that's right in front of us.
My primal mind takes over and suddenly, I am plunged
into the abyss.
I am *right* is not the same as I *understand* myself.
And *I am not* is not the answer either.

scratch pad

It takes me some time to get there.
Am I destined to love through the rear-view mirror?
Always appreciating from distances closer than they
appear.

I'm always moving so quickly,
like someone is going to take the words right out of my
mouth.

I like playing with addiction.
I'm addicted to vices that mean very little to my mind.
Maybe it's the subtle clinging to what it means to be
human.
Maybe it's my small act of relating to a world that no
longer feels relatable.

A language; written in livelihood.

The weather's changing.
The crows flock overhead once again.
And I wonder if my cat is reminded of her hometown of
San Francisco.

Today I learned that dolphins can shut off their brains
and drown themselves.
And all I can think is *what a beautiful gift*.

an ode to Robert Frost

Two roads diverged in a dark wood.
I looked down one as far as I could.
I see a *life* of wondering, but not wandering.
There is familiarity, the deepest form of love there is.
My skin is tan and I am strong.
I look into the eyes of people who know why I am the
way I am;
I am surrounded by masters of life.
New roots grow deep in this perfect wood.
I walk the labyrinth daily,
guided by ethereal beings, goddesses of the earth.

I am past the point of no return.

Down the other road lies a thick forest of the unknown.
A peaceful stillness settles overhead and I am walking
amongst the clouds;
my mind will always want to come along.
The promise of clarity that can never be taken away.
The shedding of all that is left of me in exchange for
rebirth.
This time, I'm not running.
I walk slowly, more sure of each next step,
crystalizing the wisdom we've always had.

No more checking for understanding.
Maybe then, I will be understood.

And in truth, this decision that feels like *everything* will
be worked out in the ever-changing, ever-expansive
fabric of the universe.
In ways we could never imagine.
Lost in the intricate pattern and infinite beauty,
like a snag that you didn't notice when you made the
purchase.
My mother always did.

Billy's

Things come back to you;
Like the names of people.
Like the sandwich shop my parents used to own every
time I pass the deli section of the grocery store.
Or the city you grew up in that was never really yours.
And the words you felt like you could never utter again
come flowing out of a place only you know.
And the butterfly you let go that you'll see one day,
just when you've forgotten.
Like the person you have always been and will continue
to be.
In the way your friend bakes cookies, using flax seed
egg, that awakens you to your own understanding;
you don't have to do things the way your mother always
did.
And the red in the roses reminds you of your piece in the
board game you grew up playing,
or the red chili *flakes* you put on your avocado toast that
contrasts the red chili *powder* I use for the food of my
people.

time capsules

Maybe life is the journey of re-collecting little pieces of
our soul.
The pieces we left,
scattered in the ethers.
Mini time capsules that remain ephemeral, untouched,
undiscovered.
In space, where time no longer exists,
I reach out to hold you.
Just long enough for a taste.
You see, I've lost myself before.
Pieces of me live in the eternal essence of every person
I've ever met.
When will the ball be passed back to me?

gaia

In the way shells living amongst the rocks start to imitate them.

In the way garlic almost never goes bad and tastes so vastly different depending on how it's cut.

In the way banana peels keep them safe until the moment it touches the air.

finality

I always hated the idea that "history repeats itself."
That nations rise and fall.
I wondered when this one would.
In a world where borders have held too much weight,
I feel like *Sisyphus*.
Pushing the boulder uphill isn't a punishment by the
gods; it is the meaning of life.
To learn each lesson, over and over again.
Until you've dissolved entirely and there is nothing left
but truth.

I can't be responsible for it all, but maybe *we* can.

Wake up to the beauty of the person right next to you.
Let's hold hands until nothing is broken anymore.
And our linking together is not the tower of Babel; it is
our birthright.
To see another person as yourself——in moments of
safety.

9 7 8 1 8 0 7 1 5 2 5 3 6